Bibliographic information published by the German National Library:

The German National Library lists this publication in the National Bibliography; detailed bibliographic data are available on the Internet at http://dnb.dnb.de .

Imprint:

Copyright © 2016 GRIN Verlag
Print and binding: Books on Demand GmbH, Norderstedt Germany
ISBN: 9783668382565

Anonym

Time preferences and happiness. The influence of happiness on time management

GRIN Verlag

GRIN - Your knowledge has value

Since its foundation in 1998, GRIN has specialized in publishing academic texts by students, college teachers and other academics as e-book and printed book. The website www.grin.com is an ideal platform for presenting term papers, final papers, scientific essays, dissertations and specialist books.

Visit us on the internet:

http://www.grin.com/

http://www.facebook.com/grincom

http://www.twitter.com/grin_com

Time preferences and happiness

TABLE OF CONTENTS:

1.INTRODUCTION

Regret for the things you did can be tempered by time; it is regret for the things you did not do that is inconsolable.

Sidney J. Harris

Time is a confusing issue in economics. It is well known that time has long been a subject of debate and a major source of division among economists.

Many consider happiness to be the main goal. The philosopher Aristotle writes, "Happiness is something final and self-sufficient, and is the end of an action." He assures that people strive for happiness for its own sake, because it is good and desirable. This paper try to examine whether happiness affects intertemporal decision making and investigate whether happiness decreases time preference based on a random-assignment experiment made by Ifcher John and Homa Zarghamee .

One more interesting experiment will be shown in this paper, made by David DeSteno, Ye Li, Leah Dickens, and Jennifer S. Lerner (2014). They found that the emotion gratitude reduces impatience even when real money is at stake, and the effects of gratitude are differentiable from those of the more general positive state of happiness.

Research experiment made by Guven, C. (2007) study the impact of individual self-reported happiness on individual economic decisions, such as saving, consumption, portfolio composition, migration and fertility is represented as well in this paper .

Drichoutis, A. C., & Nayga, R. M. (2013) examine the role of mood in joint elicitation of risk and time preferences.

Experiment done by Flesher, D. (2015) shows an attempt to study both the psychological and economics details of the preceding issues.

2.Definition of „time preference" and "happiness"

Time is a resource like any other. And an important one, respect for which can boost effectiveness and profitability.In economics, time preference is the relative valuation placed on a good at an earlier date compared with its valuation at a later date(Frederick S., Loewenstein G., O'donoghue T.2002). Time preferences are captured mathematically in the discount function. The higher the time preference, the higher the discount placed on returns receivable or costs payable in the future.

In general, people tend to prefer sooner, smaller rewards over the delayed rewards. The rate at which one discounts rewards over time is known as the intertemporal discount rate (Doyle, 2013). Discount rates are typically measured by deriving an equilibrium, or indifference point, between a smaller and a larger reward.

In the neoclassical theory of interest Fisher plotted the intertemporal consumption decision on a two-good indiffrence diagram, with consumption in the current year on the abscissa, and consumption in the following year on the ordinate. This representation made clear that a person's observed (marginal) rate of time preference-the marginal rate of substitution at her chosen consumption bundle-depends on two considerations: time preference and diminishing marginal utility. These two rates must necessarily be equal, and this equilibrium is brought about by the relative prices of present and future consumption..

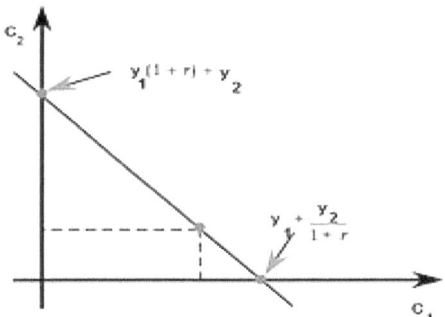

(Graph 1)Intertemporal budget constraint with consumption of period 1 and 2 on x-axis and y-axis respectively

In Fisher's formulation, pure time preference can be interpreted as the marginal rate of substitution on the diagonal, where consumption is equal in both periods (Graph 1). Fisher's writings included extensive discussions of the psychologic Fisher's formulation, pure time preference al determinants of time preference. Like Bohm-Bawerk, he differentiated "objective factors," such as projected future wealth and risk, from "personal factors." Fisher's list of personal factors included the four described by Rae, "foresight" (the ability to imagine future wants-the inverse of the deficit that Bohm-Bawerk postulated), and "fashion," which Fisher believed to be "of vast importance . . . in its influence both on the rate of interest and on the distribution of wealth itself." (Fisher 1930, p. 88):

The most fitful of the causes at work is probably fashion. This at the present time acts, on the one hand, to stimulate men to save and become very rich , and, on the other hand, to stimulate rich people to live in an ostentatious manner. (Fisher 1930, p. 87) Hence, in the early part of the twentieth century, "time preference" was viewed as an integration of various intertemporal motives.

In neoclassical economics, the rate of time preference is usually taken as a parameter in an individual's utility function which captures the trade off between consumption today and consumption in the future, and is thus exogenous and subjective.

Bohm-Bawerk's analysis of time preference was psychological, and much of his voluminous treatise, Capital and Interest, was devoted to discussions of the psychological constituents of time preference. However, whereas the early views of Rae, Senior, and Jevons explained intertemporal choices in terms of motives that are uniquely associated with time, Bohm-Bawerk began modeling intertemporal choice in the same terms as other economic tradeoffs-as a "technical" decision about allocating resources (to oneself) over different points in time, much as one would allocate resources between any two competing interests, such as housing and food.

Bohm-Bawerk said that the value of future goods diminishes as the length of time necessary for their completion increases.

He cited three reasons for this difference in value. First of all, in a growing economy, the supply of goods will always be larger in the future than it is in the present. Secondly, people have a tendency to underestimate their future needs due to carelessness and shortsightedness. Finally, entrepreneurs would rather initiate production with goods presently available, instead of waiting for future goods and delaying production.

By contrast, George Reisman says that time preference arises because of the possibility of being less able (say through injury or the effects of aging) or totally unable (through substantial incapacitation or death) to enjoy the use of goods in the future (Reismann,1996,pp 55-56). The further into the future someone considers, the less likely it is that this someone will be able to enjoy the goods as much as they can be enjoyed now. The root of time-preference in Reisman's view is an internal risk premium that is specific to the owner of the goods, in contrast to an external risk premium that is demanded when the owner invests them in a production process or lends them to another. He then points out that the scarcity of capital combined with the uncertainties he raises, means that time preference is unavoidable and hence a minimum rate of return on that capital (such as in interest and normal profit) is always going to be required by suppliers of capital.

Many economists have subsequently expressed discomfort with using the term "time preference" to include the effects of differential marginal utility arising from unequal consumption levels between time periods (see in particular Mancur Olson and Martin Bailey 1981).

An individual who faces several alternatives will choose the one that promises the greatest pleasure, or happiness. Kupfermann, Kandel, and Iversen (2000, p. 1007) express it: "Pleasure is unquestionably a key factor in controlling the motivated behaviors of humans". Classical economic thought holds that people are utility maximizers; individuals select the array of goods and activities, known as a consumption bundle, which gives them the greatest utility, subject to budget, time, and other constraints. Every good or activity has some inherent value or utility tied to it, and different individuals may derive different utilities from the same good. Thus, different people may have entirely different consumption bundles, yet still remain "rational," where rationality is indicative of choosing the consumption bundle which maximizes utility.

Happiness is a feeling of contentment, that life is just as it should be. Perfect happiness, enlightenment, comes when you have all of your needs satisfied.. Traditionally in economics, utility acts as a proxy for happiness. Goods and activities from which people derive value and enjoy comprise positive utility, which theoretically leads to happiness. Because money is a means for obtaining methods of producing utility, it is often assumed that increased income leads to increased happiness. However, research indicates this is not true. According to Perez-Truglia (2010) and Lee (2009), people acclimate to changes in income and other life circumstances through a phenomenon known as hedonic adaptation. This process explains why winners of the lottery only experience elevated happiness for brief periods of time, and after an accident, new paraplegics generally only suffer a decrease in overall happiness for a relatively brief period of time. Eventually both lottery winners and paraplegics regress back to their set point of happiness, despite the objectively different circumstances.

Most of the economics literature uses happiness and life satisfaction interchangeably but it has been argued that happiness describes better the instantaneous component of subjective well-being while life satisfaction is the more appropriate measure of its evaluative, long-term component (Deaton, 2008; Stevenson and Wolfers, 2008) (see figures 3 and 4).

3.Connection between time preference and happiness

Several paradigms exist to analyze connection between time preference and happiness , often with contradictory results.In one study was found out that a person who is more capable of integrating information into one's lifestyle may be more likely to be happy, as that person may have better life outcomes than those who disregard information. Many of life's choices consider around questions of time: work now and socialize later or socialize now and work later; eat healthy now and relax later or do nothing now and workout later; browse the internet now and wake up tired or go to sleep now and wake up rested; spend money now and budget more tightly later or save now and indulge later. These types of decisions all largely condense to one main idea: does one do something now that has an immediate positive consequence associated with it, or does one engage in an activity that has a potentially larger, later reward associated with it?

Although there are evaluative decisions, such as career paths and interpersonal issues, the daily decision making largely focuses on whether or not one delays gratification. Different people face these types of decisions differently; some tend to prefer the instant gratification, whereas others tend to hold off for the larger reward later. The extent to which people prefer sooner rewards rather than later, larger

rewards reflects what is known as time preference, temporal discounting, and delay of gratification, depending on the domain. In general, people tend to prefer sooner, smaller rewards over the delayed rewards. The rate at which one discounts rewards over time is known as the intertemporal discount rate (Doyle, 2013). Discount rates are typically measured by deriving an equilibrium, or indifference point, between a smaller, immediate reward and a later, larger reward. Then, one can calculate the rate at which one discounts the future.

The tone of research is that the more one can opt for the later, larger reward, the

better (Frederick, Loewenstein, & O'Donoghue, 2002). Often, the same holds for advice the advice- givers in life dole out: do homework before going out, save money now for more money in the future, be healthy now to be healthier in the future. However, people do not always follow such advice, and often people prefer the lesser, immediate reward (Mischel, Ebbesen, & Zeiss, 1972). Because of the vast variety of intertemporal choices one must make, an exploration of the interplay of discounting and one's overall wellbeing, or happiness, could provide meaningful insight into human behavior.

Many consider happiness to be the ultimate goal. The philosopher Aristotle writes, "Happiness is something final and self-sufficient, and is the end of an action." He argues people strive for happiness for its own sake, because it is inherently good and desirable. According to Schoch (2006), utilitarian philosophers Jeremy Bentham and John Stuart Mill assert the optimal society is the one which maximizes happiness, i.e., creating the most happiness for the most people. Even the Declaration of Independence (1776) cites the "pursuit of happiness" as one of the premiere rights of individuals. Although many disagree about what truly begets happiness, the underlying theme that happiness is good and an important, if not supreme, part of human existence is consistent across an array of philosophies.

There are two ways to view a potential relationship between happiness and time preference: first, happiness effects time preference, and second, time preference affects happiness. Both perspectives are considered for this research. Ifcher and Zarghamee (2011) provided much of the basis for the happiness affects discounting perspective. According to their analysis of the General Social Survey (1973,1974, 1976) there is correlational evidence that people who agreed more with "live for today" statements (suggesting a higher discount rate) tended to be less happy, even when controlled by factors such as age, gender, income, education, and health.

However, the General Social Survey only has one item for happiness and one than appears to indicate discounting tendencies, rather than true attempts to quantify either variable.

Ifcher and Zarghamee (2011) provided some additional proof of the effects of positive affect on temporal discounting, as they tested participants by inducing a positive mood using comedy clips and found that those in the positive affect group had lower discount rates than those in the control group.Moreover, according to Ifcher and Zarghamee, a study by Baumeister, Bratslavsky, and Tice (1998) found that positive affect increased time spent studying for a test with no rewards. Additionally, Isen and Reeve (2005) found that positive affect increased intrinsic motivation. Furthermore, Guven (2012) proposed that happiness affects discounting. According to that research, individual happiness impacted economic decision-making. Through using the positive correlation between sunshine and happiness, Guven found that when people saved more and spent less when happier, as caused by the good weather.Moreover, happy people evaluated decisions more, and exhibited more self-control. However, since Guven uses sunshine as a for happiness, the research may have measured more positive affect, or a state of mind rather than the feature of happiness into which the current study delves.

4.EMPIRICAL EVIDENCE

The effect of happiness on time preference (in experiment made by Ifcher John and Homa Zarghamee) was examined in laboratory experiments conducted at Santa Clara University with 69 Santa Clara undergraduates-subjects (see Table 1).

The experiment was conducted 45 minutes, and subjects received an average of $24 for their participation. First, subjects were told that the 30 time-preference questions would be of the following form: "What amount of money, $p, if paid to you today would make you indifferent to $m paid to you in t days?" where m and t would be specified.

To study the direction of causation in the relationship between happiness and time preference, Ifcher John and Homa Zarghamee attempted to exogenously control happiness. Specifically, it was attempted to manipulate subjects' mood by showing them a short film clip (Robin Williams – Live on Broadway). Watching the positive-affect clip made subjects significantly more likely to answer "happier."(see Figure 1)

As in Benhabib, Bisin, and Schotter (2010), discounting was represented by D, the factor that, when multiplied by m, yields the dollar amount p necessary today to make one indifferent to $m in t days: $D = p/m$.

Table 2 presents observed values of D for all (m, t)-combinations; Table 2A pools all subjects, and Tables 2B and 2C present the treatment and control groups, respectively. Subjects consistently reduce the distant future more heavily than they do the near future. The findings showed that the positive mood-inducement increases the present value of a delayed payment in theirs experiment.Depending on the future payment and specification, the magnitude of the effect ranges from 4% (specification (4), $m = 51.71) and 27% (specification (8), $m = 11.56) of the future payment.

In this experiment , they successfully improved subjects' mood . Results from this experiment indicate that subjects in the treatment group exhibit significantly lower
time preference than do subjects in the control group.

One more interesting experiment was done by David DeSteno, Ye Li, Leah Dickens, and Jennifer S. Lerner (2014).The human mind tends to excessively discount the value of delayed rewards relative to immediate ones.They found evidence supporting this alternative view. Particularly, they found that the emotion gratitude reduces impatience even when real money is at stake, and the effects of gratitude are differentiable from those of the more general positive state of happiness. The findings find out that thankfulness reduces excessive economic impatience. These research challenge the opinion that individuals must tamp down

8

affective responses through effortful self-regulation to reach more patient and adaptive economic decisions.

Another research experiment was made by Guven, C. (2007) using data from DNB Household Survey from Netherlands (Figure 2). This experiment studied the impact of individual self-reported happiness on individual economic decisions, such as saving, consumption, portfolio composition, migration and fertility. This study shows that unexpected increases in daily sunshine and unexpected wins in soccer increase happiness but individual happiness is not very persistent over time (table 4). Instrumenting individual happiness with sunshine, lagged happiness or soccer results, the experiment finds that happy people do smoke less and use less alcohol (Tables 5 and 6). Also interesting to know , happy people save more and spend less. In addition, they also plan to save more and spend less in the future. This experiment shows us that marginal propensity to consume is lower for the happy people (Table 7). Happy people do not use internet banking as much and have much more control over their investments (Table 8).

Drichoutis, A. C., & Nayga, R. M. (2013) tested whether induced mood states have an effect on elicited risk and time preferences. In their study, they examined the role of mood in joint elicitation of risk and time preferences. They revisited the issue of determining the effect of mood states on risk and time preferences. In their work they explore if a cognitively demanding task right after mood inducement could affect risk preferences and whether there are gender differences in elicited risk and time preferences.

They used a lot of literature in study that relates mood states with risk or time preferences. In Drichoutis A. C., & Nayga study, although they find some differences in risk preferences between subjects in the control, positive mood, and negative mood treatments. They find evidence that a same-gender environment can transform risk preferences (but not discount rates) for females (but not males).

One more example experiment was done by Flesher, D. (Happiness and Time Preference:2015) . The tone of research was that the more one can opt for the later, larger reward, the better (Frederick, Loewenstein, & O'Donoghue, 2002).This research was an attempt to study both the psychological and economics details of the preceding issues. Through experimental observation and measurement of individual discount rates and levels of happiness, the underlying psychological components of temporal discounting and its relationship with happiness were examined, as well as incorporating that into different models of economic behavior.

Daniel Flesher tried to find the answers to the following questions in his work:

1) Research Question One: Do individuals discount periods of happiness differently than money?

2)Research Question Two: Is there a connection between the extent to which someone discounts the future and their happiness?

3)Research Question Three: Does being told about the positive effects of low discount rates and the adverse effects of high discount rates change individuals' indicated temporal preferences?

4)Research Question Four: How does the type of discounting model affect the interpretations and economics importance of the results?

Using a wide range of different experiments he shows different results and opinions.

5.CONCLUSION

The connection between happiness and discounting may go a long way in terms of explaining differences in life outcomes between individuals. The people who tend to discount less have better life outcomes and are thus happier.

Many consider happiness to be a premiere force in life, if not the ultimate force.

The experiments result has implications for the effect of happiness on time preference and the role of emotions in economic decision making, in general.

The findings indicate that the happy mood inducement significantly reduces time preferences.That is, the positive mood-inducement increases the present value of a delayed payment. The relationship between happiness and time preference is presumably causal with increased happiness reducing time preference. This finding is important since time preference increases the likelihood of a host of negative outcomes, for example, overconsumption, addiction, reduced human capital accumulation, and diminished saving.

Experiment done by David DeSteno, Ye Li, Leah Dickens, and Jennifer S. Lerner (2014) have found the evidence that the human mind tends to excessively discount the value of delayed rewards relative to immediate ones. The research findings find out that thankfulness reduces excessive economic impatience.

Guven, C. (2007) study shows that unexpected increases in daily sunshine and unexpected wins in soccer increase happiness but individual happiness is not very persistent over time (table 4). He shows a lot of examples in his work.

Drichoutis, A. C., & Nayga, R. M. (2013) explored if a cognitively demanding task right after mood inducement could affect risk preferences and whether there are gender differences in elicited risk and time preferences.

Flesher, D. (2015) has studied the psychological and economics details of the preceding issues. He examined underlying psychological components of temporal discounting and its relationship with happiness .

6.REFERENCES

DeSteno, David, et al. "Gratitude a tool for reducing economic impatience." *Psychological science* (2014): 0956797614529979.

Doyle, J. R. (2013). Survey of time preference, delay discounting models.*Judgment and Decision Making, 8*(2), 116.

Drichoutis, A. C., & Nayga, R. M. (2013). Eliciting risk and time preferences under induced mood states. *The Journal of Socio-Economics, 45*, 18-27.

Fisher, I. (1930). The Theory of Interest Macmillan. *New York.*

Flesher, D. (2015). Happiness and Time Preference: An Empirical Analysis of Individual Happiness and Information on Intertemporal Choice and Delaying Gratification.

Frederick, S., Loewenstein, G., & O'donoghue, T. (2002). Time discounting and time preference: A critical review. *Journal of economic literature, 40*(2), 351-401.

Frey, B. S., & Benesch, C. (2008). TV, time, and happiness. *Homo Oeconomicus, 25*(4-5), 413-424.

George, R. (1996). Capitalism: A treatise on economics.

Guven, C. (2012). Reversing the question: Does happiness affect consumption and savings behavior?. *Journal of Economic Psychology, 33*(4), 701-717.

Ifcher, J., & Zarghamee, H. (2011). Happiness and Time Preference: The Effect of Positive Affect in a Random-Assignment Exper. *The American Economic Review, 101*(7), 3109-3129.

Ikeda, S., Kato, H. K., Ohtake, F., & Tsutsui, Y. (Eds.). (2016). *Behavioral Economics of Preferences, Choices, and Happiness.* Springer.

Lelkes, O. (2007). Happiness over the life-cycle: Exploring age-specific preferences. *Mainstreaming Ageing: Indicators to Monitor Sustainable Policies, European Centre Vienna, Ashgate: Aldershot (UK).*

Kupfermann, I., Kandel, E. R., & Iversen, S. (2000). Motivational and addictive states. *Principles of neural science, 4.*

Mancini, M., & Mancini, M. (2003). *Time management.* New York: McGraw-Hill...

Netzer, N. (2009). Evolution of time preferences and attitudes toward risk. *The American Economic Review, 99*(3), 937-955.

O'Driscoll, G. P., Rizzo, M. J., & Garrison, R. W. (1996). *The economics of time and ignorance*. Psychology Press.

Olson, M., & Bailey, M. J. (1981). Positive time preference. *The Journal of Political Economy*, 1-25.

Robinson, J. (1980). Time in economic theory. *Kyklos, 33*(2), 219-229..

Schoch, R. (2006). *The secrets of happiness: Three thousand years of searching for the good life*. Simon and Schuster.

Shackle, G. L. S. (1967). *Time in economics*. North-Holland Publishing Company. Strulik, H. (2015). Preferences, income, and life satisfaction: An equivalence result. *Mathematical Social Sciences, 75*, 20-26.

Wunder, C., & Heineck, G. (2013). Working time preferences, hours mismatch and well-being of couples: Are there spillovers?. *Labour Economics, 24*, 244-252.

7.APPENDICES

APPENDIX

TABLE A1—RESULTS FROM REGRESSING "LIVE FOR TODAY" ON SELF-REPORTED HAPPINESS

Dependent variable: Live for today (1 = "agree" and 0 = "disagree")	(1)	(2)
Happiness (3 = "very happy," 2 = "pretty happy," and 1 = "not too happy")	−0.048***	−0.042**
	(0.012)	(0.021)
Age	—	−0.006
		(0.006)
Age squared	—	0.000
		(0.000)
Attend religious services at least once per month	—	0.010
		(0.026)
Female	—	0.062**
		(0.028)
Income below median (< $15,000)	—	0.073**
		(0.035)
Low education (< 11 years)	—	0.216***
		(0.032)
Nonwhite	—	0.123***
		(0.045)
Poor or fair health	—	0.073**
		(0.036)
Observations	1,636	1,636

Note: Standard errors reported in parentheses.
    ***Significant at the 1 percent level.
     **Significant at the 5 percent level.
      *Significant at the 10 percent level.

Table A1. Ifcher, J., & Zarghamee, H. (2011)

Panel A. $D(m, t)$, holding m constant, pooled data

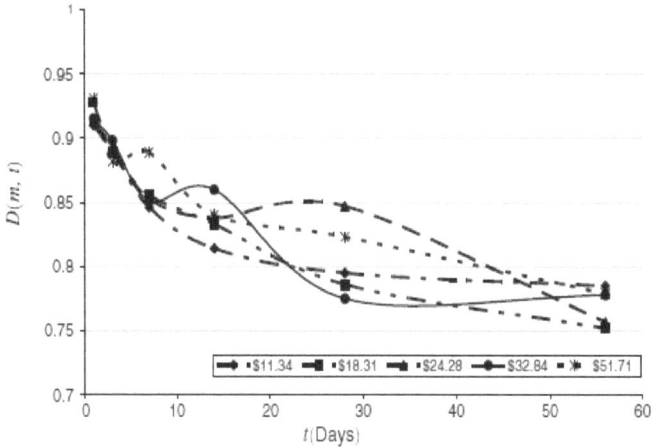

Panel B. $D(m, t)$, averaging over m, by treatment, where avg = average, tr = treatment, and c = control

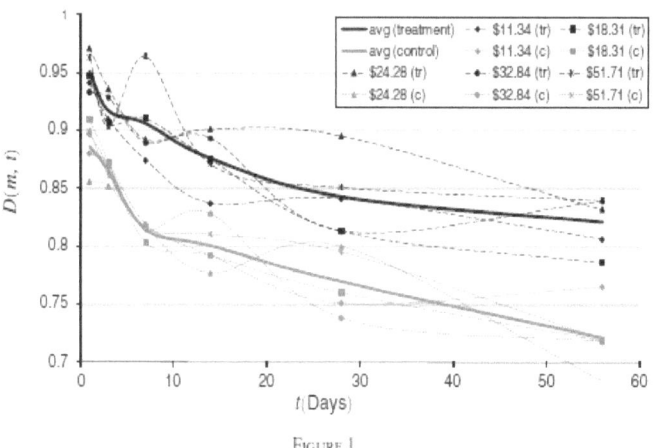

Figure I

Figure 1. Ifcher, J., & Zarghamee, H. (2011)

Figure 2 Province level Happiness in Netherlands (Deaton, 2008)

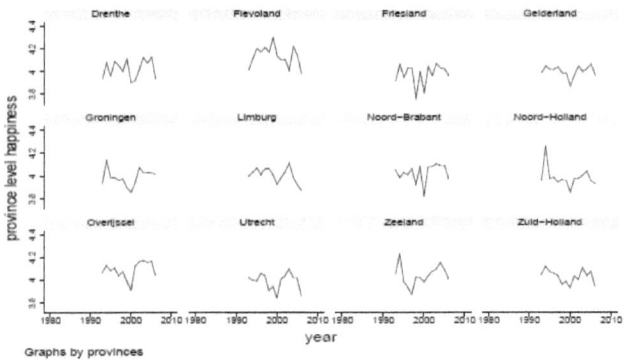

Figure 3 Global data on the correlation between income and life satisfaction from Gallup World Poll – Deaton (2008)

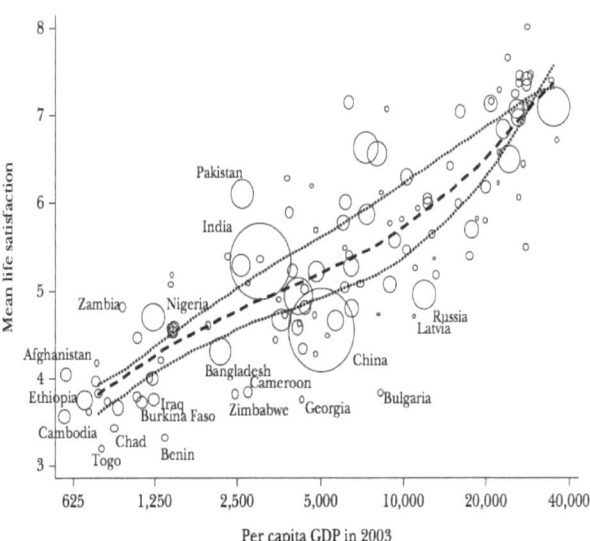

Figure 4 Distribution of estimates of the within-country life satisfaction-income gradient from Gallup World Poll – Stevenson & Wolfers (2008)

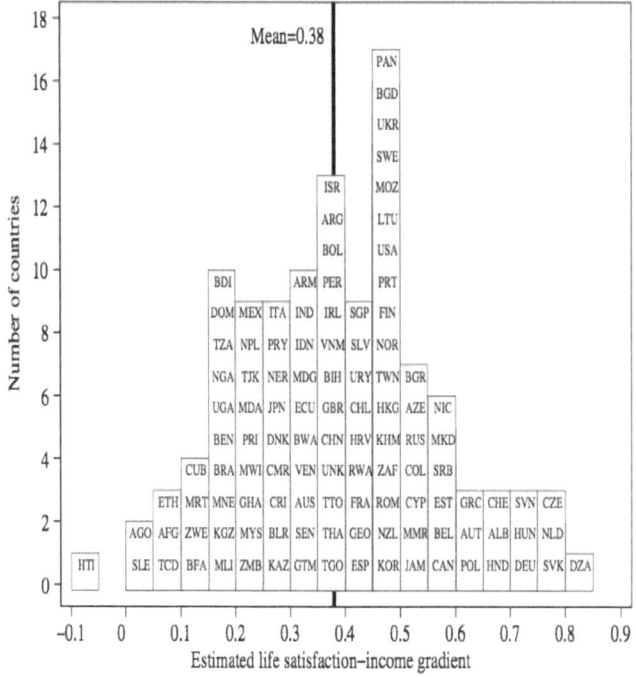

TABLE 2A– $D(m,t)$, POOLED DATA, 69 SUBJECTS

m(Dollars)	1	3	7	14	28	56	Mean
$11.34	0.910 (0.215)	0.890 (0.171)	0.846 (0.203)	0.814 (0.210)	0.795 (0.238)	0.766[a] (0.260)	0.837[a] (0.223)
$18.31	0.928 (0.200)	0.889 (0.195)	0.856 (0.217)	0.833 (0.207)	0.786 (0.235)	0.752 (0.272)	0.841 (0.229)
$24.28	0.910[b] (0.221)	0.893 (0.201)	0.853 (0.227)	0.838 (0.209)	0.847 (0.169)	0.757 (0.253)	0.849[b] (0.219)
$32.84	0.915 (0.211)	0.898 (0.177)	0.851 (0.219)	0.857[a] (0.160)	0.775 (0.252)	0.778 (0.244)	0.846[a] (0.219)
$51.71	0.931 (0.212)	0.882 (0.241)	0.889 (0.248)	0.840 (0.258)	0.823 (0.246)	0.779 (0.265)	0.857 (0.249)
Mean	0.919[b] (0.211)	0.890 (0.197)	0.859 (0.222)	0.836[a] (0.211)	0.805 (0.230)	0.766[a] (0.258)	0.846[c] (0.228)

Note: Standard errors reported in parentheses.
[a] One missing response.
[b] Three missing responses.
[c] Five missing responses.

TABLE 2B– $D(m,t)$, TREATMENT GROUP, 34 SUBJECTS

m(Dollars)	1	3	7	14	28	56	Mean
$11.34	0.941 (0.167)	0.909 (0.123)	0.874 (0.159)	0.837 (0.214)	0.841 (0.198)	0.806 (0.246)	0.868 (0.192)
$18.31	0.947 (0.157)	0.906 (0.184)	0.910 (0.131)	0.875 (0.149)	0.813 (0.232)	0.786 (0.258)	0.873 (0.197)
$24.28	0.968[b] (0.071)	0.936 (0.115)	0.892 (0.160)	0.901 (0.114)	0.895 (0.131)	0.832 (0.203)	0.903[b] (0.143)
$32.84	0.933 (0.173)	0.928 (0.107)	0.889 (0.159)	0.889[a] (0.129)	0.813 (0.224)	0.839 (0.213)	0.882[a] (0.176)
$51.71	0.963 (0.171)	0.903 (0.211)	0.964 (0.053)	0.871 (0.209)	0.851 (0.231)	0.840 (0.222)	0.899 (0.197)
Mean	0.950[b] (0.152)	0.917 (0.153)	0.906 (0.141)	0.875[a] (0.168)	0.843 (0.206)	0.821 (0.228)	0.885[c] (0.182)

Note: Standard errors reported in parentheses.
[a] One missing response.
[b] Two missing responses.
[c] Three missing responses.

TABLE 2C–D(m, t), CONTROL GROUP, 35 SUBJECTS

m(Dollars)	t(Days)						
	1	3	7	14	28	56	Mean
$11.34	0.880	0.871	0.819	0.792	0.751	0.725[a]	0.807[a]
	(0.252)	(0.208)	(0.237)	(0.208)	(0.268)	(0.356)	(0.246)
$18.31	0.909	0.873	0.803	0.792	0.760	0.719	0.809
	(0.235)	(0.206)	(0.268)	(0.246)	(0.239)	(0.284)	(0.253)
$24.28	0.856[a]	0.852	0.816	0.777	0.800	0.684	0.798[a]
	(0.292)	(0.253)	(0.274)	(0.258)	(0.190)	(0.277)	(0.263)
$32.84	0.897	0.869	0.815	0.828	0.738	0.718	0.811
	(0.243)	(0.223)	(0.261)	(0.182)	(0.274)	(0.259)	(0.248)
$51.71	0.897	0.861	0.816	0.810	0.795	0.720	0.817
	(0.243)	(0.268)	(0.330)	(0.299)	(0.260)	(0.293)	(0.286)
Mean	0.889[a]	0.865	0.814	0.800	0.769	0.713[a]	0.808[b]
	(0.251)	(0.230)	(0.272)	(0.240)	(0.246)	(0.274)	(0.259)

Note: Standard errors reported in parentheses.
[a] One missing response.
[b] Two missing responses.

TABLE 2D–{$D_{Treatment}(m, t) - D_{Control}(m, t)$}, 34 SUBJECTS IN TREATMENT GROUP,
35 SUBJECTS IN CONTROL GROUP

m(Dollars)	t(Days)						
	1	3	7	14	28	56	Mean
$11.34	0.061	0.039	0.055	0.045	0.091	0.080[a]	0.055
	(0.052)	(0.041)	(0.049)	(0.051)	(0.057)	(0.063)	(0.037)
$18.31	0.038	0.034	0.107**	0.082*	0.053	0.067	0.063
	(0.048)	(0.047)	(0.051)	(0.049)	(0.057)	(0.065)	(0.041)
$24.28	0.111***ᵇ	0.083*	0.076	0.125**	0.094**	0.149**	0.111***
	(0.051)	(0.048)	(0.054)	(0.048)	(0.039)	(0.059)	(0.039)
$32.84	0.036	0.059	0.074	0.060ᵇ	0.074	0.122**	0.072*
	(0.051)	(0.042)	(0.052)	(0.038)	(0.060)	(0.057)	(0.040)
$51.71	0.064	0.043	0.149**	0.061	0.055	0.120*	0.082
	(0.051)	(0.058)	(0.057)	(0.062)	(0.059)	(0.063)	(0.050)
Mean	0.065	0.051	0.092**	0.076*	0.073	0.099*	0.081**
	(0.046)	(0.042)	(0.046)	(0.041)	(0.046)	(0.052)	(0.039)

Note: Standard errors reported in parentheses.
*** Significant at the 1 percent level.
** Significant at the 5 percent level.
* Significant at the 10 percent level.
[a] One missing observation in control group.
[b] Two missing observations in treatment group.

Tables 2C-D and 2D Ifcher, J., & Zarghamee, H. (2011)

TABLE 3—RESULTS OF ESTIMATING EQUATION (1)
(Dependent variable is present value, p)

	(1)	(2)	(3)	(4)	(5)	(6)	(7)	(8)
Treatment	2.202*	2.012**	2.337**	2.416**	2.997**	3.027**	3.028**	3.507***
	(1.124)	(0.958)	(1.100)	(1.002)	(1.352)	(1.159)	(1.265)	(1.207)
Only discounter included	—	—	—	—	Yes	Yes	Yes	Yes
College	—	Yes	—	Yes	—	Yes	—	Yes
Gender	—	Yes	—	Yes	—	Yes	—	Yes
Race	—	Yes	—	Yes	—	Yes	—	Yes
Religion	—	Yes	—	Yes	—	Yes	—	Yes
Practicing	—	Yes	—	Yes	—	Yes	—	Yes
Income	—	Yes	—	Yes	—	Yes	—	Yes
Self-reported happiness	—	—	Yes	Yes	—	—	Yes	Yes
Excludes observations, where $p = m$	—	—	—	—	Yes	Yes	Yes	Yes
R^2	0.748	0.794	0.751	0.795	0.680	0.744	0.683	0.745
Observations	2,065	2,035	2,065	2,035	1,471	1,447	1,471	1,447
Clusters	69	68	69	68	58	57	58	57

Notes: Robust standard errors reported in parentheses. For five observations, the reported value of p was unintelligible and thus excluded from all specifications. Columns 2, 4, 6, and 8 have one fewer cluster, and up to 30 fewer observations, than columns 1, 3, 5, and 7, respectively, because one subject had unreported demographic characteristics. Columns 5–8 exclude observations where $p = m$. Ten subjects had $p = m$ for all observations; thus there are ten fewer clusters in 5–8 than in 1–4.

***Significant at the 1 percent level.
**Significant at the 5 percent level.
*Significant at the 10 percent level.

Table 3 Ifcher, J., & Zarghamee, H. (2011)

Table 4 Sunshine and Happiness Guven, C. (2007)

Dependent Variable: Self-Reported Happiness

	coef.	t-stat.
duration of daily sunshine:		
last 10 day moving average	0.001	2.2
deviation from the mean	0.004	5.1
maximum duration daily of sunshine:		
last 10 day moving average	0.004	3.4
deviation from the mean	0.006	5.1
daily cloud cover:		
last 10 day moving average	−0.048	3.4
deviation from the mean	−0.061	3.8

Notes: The ordered logit regression of self-reported happiness on controls and measures of sunshine. Every row shows the results from a different regression. Happiness is a categorical variable taking values from 1-5. Measures of sunshine are province level daily sunshine variables taken from weather stations. First rows are the weighted moving average of the last 10 days sunshine measure. Second rows are the deviation of the first row from the average of the first row in the last 60 years. Controls for every regression are: labor force status, marital and health status, log income, number of children, number of household members, age, province fixed effects and year fixed effects.

Table 5 Happiness and Smoking Cigarettes, Guven, C. (2007)

Dependent Variable: Number of Cigarettes

instrument	OLS no	IV lagged happiness	IV sunshine
happy	−0.05**	−0.12**	−1.63
health	−0.04***	−0.06***	0.35
married(marriage settlement)	0.06*	0.12**	0.05
divorced	0.07	0.10	−0.40
living with partner(not married)	0.00	−0.06	−0.12
widowed	−0.00	0.05	−0.55
never married	−0.05	−0.01	−0.61
male	0.06***		0.03
female		−0.05*	
R-squared	0.02	0.04	.
N. of obs.	4886	2318	4024

Notes: Dependent Variable is a binary variable taking 0 if respondent smokes less than 20 cigarettes a day and 1 otherwise. Probit and Logit regressions give the same results with OLS. Health and Happiness are categorical variables taking values 1-5 but treated as continuous variables here. Additional controls: number of kids, work status, number of household members, education, income, and age are not reported since they are insignificant in all specifications. Regressions also include year and province fixed effects. For marital status, married (community of property) is excluded. ***, **, * denotes 1%, 5%, and 10% significance, respectively.

Table 6 Happiness and Drinking Behavior, Guven, C. (2007)

Dependent Variable:Alcohol

instrument	OLS no	IV lagged happiness	IV sunshine
happy	−0.01***	−0.03***	−0.14
married(marriage settlement)	0.02**	0.02*	0.03**
divorced	0.04**	0.04*	−0.00
living with partner(not married)	0.01	0.00	0.01
widowed	−0.00	−0.00	−0.03
never married	0.01	0.01	-0.02
income	0.00***	0.00***	0.00***
male	0.08***	0.07***	0.07***
R-squared	0.03	0.02	.
N. of obs.	21475	10943	17426

Notes: Dependent Variable is a bivariate variable, refers to "no","yes", which is the answer to the question "On average, do you have more than 4 alcoholic drinks a day?" Probit and Logit regressions give the same results with OLS. Health and Happiness are categorical variables taking values 1-5 but treated as continuous variables here. Additional controls: number of kids, work status, number of household members, education, health, and age are not reported since they are insignificant in all specifications. Regressions also include year and province fixed effects. For marital status, married (community of property) is excluded.***, **, * denotes 1%, 5%, and 10% significance, respectively.

Table 7 Happiness and Marginal Propensity to Consume, Guven, C. (2007)

Dependent Variable:Marginal Propensity to Consume

instrument	OLS no	IV lagged happiness	IV sunshine
happy	0.07***	0.11**	2.95*
health	0.03*	0.03	−0.63*
married(marriage settlement)	0.05	0.08	−0.07
divorced	−0.01	0.03	0.93*
living with partner(not married)	−0.03	−0.08	0.11
widowed	−0.14*	−0.13	0.66
never married	−0.09*	−0.09	0.72*
number of household members	−0.03	−0.05	−0.27*
number of children	0.05	0.05	0.34*
education	−0.01*	−0.02***	−0.00
age	0.01***	0.01***	0.01***
male	0.04*	0.06**	0.20*
R-squared	0.02	0.02	.
N. of obs.	21005	10682	17027

Notes: Dependent Variable is a categorical variable from 1-7, which is the answer to the question "Some people spend all their income immediately. Others save some money in order to have something to fall back on. Please indicate what you do with money that is left over after having paid for food, rent, and other necessities on a scale from 1 to 7, where 1 means "I like to spend all my money immediately" and 7 means "I want to save as much as possible". Ordered Probit and Ordered Logit regressions give the same results with OLS. Health and Happiness are categorical variables taking values 1-5 but treated as continuous variables here. Additional controls: work status, and income are not reported since they are insignificant in all specifications. Regressions also include year and province fixed effects. For marital status, married (community of property) is excluded.***, **, * denotes 1%, 5%, and 10% significance, respectively.

Table 8 Happiness and Internet Banking Usage, Guven, C. (2007)

Dependent Variable:Frequency of Internet Banking Usage

instrument	OLS no	IV lagged happiness	IV sunshine
happy	0.07*	0.16*	−2.21*
health	0.00	−0.02	0.60*
married(marriage settlement)	0.18*	0.20*	0.24*
divorced	0.13	0.29	−0.61
living with partner(not married)	0.23**	0.34***	0.39**
widowed	0.07	0.24	−0.75
never married	0.01	0.09	−0.70*
education	−0.02*	−0.00	−0.03
income	0.00***	0.00***	0.00***
age	−0.02***	−0.02***	−0.01***
male	0.29***	0.31***	
female			−0.10
R-squared	0.06	0.08	.
N. of obs.	4773	3344	3974

Notes: Dependent Variable is a categorical variable from 1-5, which is the answer to the question "Nowadays, a number of banks offer the possibility to arrange banking affairs through Internet, without the mediation of a person. Do you use such a facility? 1. no 2. yes, very rarely 3. yes, every now and then 4. yes, often 5. yes, very often". Ordered Probit and Ordered Logit regressions give the same results with OLS. Health and Happiness are categorical variables taking values 1-5 but treated as continuous variables here. Number of household members and number of children are insignificant in all specifications.Regressions also include year and province fixed effects. For marital status, married (community of property) is excluded.***, **, * denotes 1%, 5%, and 10% significance, respectively.